It's A Won

What You Make ~~Up to You~~

CW01494931

By The Yeoman Poet
(George Greig)

Copyright © 2023 George Greig

ISBN: 978-1-916596-95-5

All rights reserved, including the right to reproduce this book, or portions thereof in any form. No part of this text may be reproduced, transmitted, downloaded, decompiled, reverse engineered, or stored, in any form or introduced into any information storage and retrieval system, in any form or by any means, whether electronic or mechanical without the express written permission of the author.

Foreword – by the Poet

Growing older is a genuine privilege and the ability to look back on a long life is empowering. You can recall your failings, your successes, make adjustments after the fact, and actually get the chance to get it right next time around. Many folks don't get this golden opportunity, nor the chance to give their life meaning through acts of kindness, teaching others before they make the same mistakes, or simply trying to make a difference.

I have loved words throughout my life, and they have enriched my life in so many ways, from just being a storyteller in school, to crafting eulogies for lost comrades and through that, relieving the terrible despair of loss. As a child, I was advised to become a writer, but whilst I didn't listen, I never stopped writing throughout my career. It was a strength that set me apart, as a soldier and as a businessman, enhancing and complimenting other skills as I made my way through life.

Strangely, as a long serving military man, I also love poetry which I believe to be nothing more than an extension of storytelling; another communication channel that can deliver stories with great clarity and brevity. Despite my roots as a Highland Scot, it has taken me a lifetime to realise that Rabbie Burns did share some incredible foresight, compassion, and human decency when he said, "*A man's A Man For A' That*". Simply meaning "*A man's value isn't defined by how much he owns, it's much deeper*", or his conviction that "*One day the world will change, and all men will Brothers Be*".

As I have aged, I have come to realise that our lives are defined by the simpler things we do. Stopping to listen to a homeless person's story, giving people a second chance, showing them some respect, or just providing some support can be very rewarding.

My reason for bringing these 80 poems together is to make the most of an opportunity to share my personal life lessons, beliefs, and values whilst acknowledging that I have got some stuff right, some wrong, but wanting mostly to share the good bits and just give a little back. I hope my stories are of interest and that they might make those who read them realise *"It's a wonderful life, what you make of it is up to you"*.

Contents

1. What Do You Want From Life?

Have you ever considered just what you want from life?
is it simply a family, a job, your health and no strife.
Or do you have a dream that sits deep in your heart,
to do something special that will set you apart.

If you don't have a dream, you must ask yourself why,
life's not a rehearsal you need to give it a try.
We are all special and have something to give,
if you don't, you'll regret it for as long as you live.

When you decide what it is that's right for you,
it will lift you, excite you and focus what you do.
Don't be put off by naysayers or negative vibes,
people that do this have wasted their lives.

Be positive, strong and give it all that you've got,
that's how you'll make things happen and achieve a lot.
You'll shine and be an example to those who said it can't be
done,
and be proud that you showed you've got what it takes, you
won.

*A lot of people just don't know what they want from life and
that's a shame. Knowing what you want gives you purpose and
something to plan for; it doesn't mean that your path can't
change as your life develops. Do things that make you happy,
that make you feel fulfilled, and that allows you to be the best
you can be.*

*What do you want from life and how do you plan to achieve it.
You need a plan. If you want a little inspiration, contact me, I'd
love to help.*

2. Fame & Fortune

It isn't all about the money and it's not about the fame,
there's a lot more to think about in life's little game.
Do others matter, or is it all just about you,
or is your life a measure of what you can really do.

Many great people do things for free, no hidden agenda or
claim it was me!
for others they do nothing unless everyone knows, it's there for
all to see.
They seek the riches and a lust for fame drives them on,
but as seen so many times, they get success then they're quickly
gone.

We live in a world where everybody wants to be famous or
great,
they don't want to work at it of course, that's the bit they hate.
A quick turn on BGT or even I'm a celeb,
it's the quick route they want, the one for any pleb.

If life was as shallow as this, I would struggle to see the point
behind it,
there's so much more for all of us, you just need to do your bit.
Satchmo said it's a wonderful life and there's no doubt that's
true,
all that's required is for you to define just what you want to do.

Don't be fooled into thinking fame and fortune are all that matter in life. Health, happiness, and contentment will always win out, and great legacies can be created from doing good things. Showing respect, empathy and care for others will set you apart and to be blunt, nothing feels quite as special as helping another human being overcome adversity. Try it.

Do you have a "goal"; if so, who have you told about it and what's it going to achieve? How is it helping others?

3. Industry

The rules of industry run very deep, of that there is no doubt,
if you aren't on the board or a senior guy, then sadly you have
no clout.
Bright and committed with a lot to say, you have no platform to
use,
because you're just a worker, not a manager with something to
lose.

Before I entered the commercial world, I thought I would see
care and compassion,
but the world I encountered wasn't this way, dog eat dog was
the fashion.
That's where I decided my role would be, to show what can be
achieved,
when treating all with respect, empathy and showing they were
believed.

People are everything, so take care of your staff,
don't treat them with disrespect as you sit there having a laugh.
Often driven by selfishness and personal interest I know,
many boards are inept, and their members should go.

The lack of moral courage is often rife at the top,
it's easier to deflect things or simply lie if someone has a pop.
Without their team a boss can't succeed, and the business will
surely fail,
it's a very simple point you'd think, it should be easy for them
to nail.

Before I entered industry, I held a rather naïve view that empathy, care, and compassion would feature very highly on the list of key people skills for leaders and managers; how wrong I was! Whereas these things sit at the heart of my training and profession as a soldier, I found them to be sadly lacking in the commercial world.

I must admit, my constant reference to these attributes, and their implementation across every department or business I have led, set me apart, facilitating the building of some remarkable relationships and teams. What difference are you going to make?

4. Building a Life

When you come from nothing you must never accept or think,
that you don't have a chance to make it to the brink.
You need to work hard, but so do we all,
if you take up the challenge, you can knock down any wall.

Work hard at school because the opportunities are there,
not just for rich kids, but people like you from anywhere.
The teachers will always help, push you to study and read,
they like to see grafters and to help them succeed.

Life isn't fair, but that's just a cliché that too many share,
if you believe in yourself and work hard, you will always get
there.
Be proud and stand strong, don't let the pressure get you down,
you don't want people thinking you're some kind of clown.

When you have built the life that you want, then you will know,
that it didn't come easy, your effort made it so.
You built the life you wanted, you can hold your head up high,
you didn't just stand there and let life pass you by.

*I am passionate about carrying a very clear message to
anybody that will listen. "Don't let anybody tell you that you
can't do something". If you believe in
yourself, show commitment and dedication, and work hard
there is very little you can't achieve, fact!*

*I also urge those from a less privileged background to ignore
negativity aimed towards them in an attempt to curb their
dreams. Yes, you can is the only message you should listen to!*

5. Where Does The Hate Come From?

I have travelled the world as a soldier, trying to bring peace and
goodwill,
but many a journey has been wasted because there is hatred
still.
Where does it come from and what can we do,
I have asked myself this often and now I'm asking you.

Why does religion or culture create such a divide?
between people who often are on the same side.
One-minute friends, who show compassion and care,
the next only hatred is seen to be there.

Often little things that shouldn't matter,
change lives for ever and cause people to scatter.
Never to return to the lands they have shared,
with those that forced them out, with whom it can't be repaired.

This type of hate is often ingrained, and the smallest thing can
ignite the fire,
former friends and neighbours turn on each other, the results are
often dire.
Where does the hatred come from is the question I ask,
we need to remove it but are we up to the task.

I absolutely hate racism of any kind and believe it has been behind some of the worst atrocities committed by mankind. I have created my own saying that I took from the words of Rabbie Burns, "A man's a man for a' that", which I interpret as "The colour of a person's skin has no relevance whatsoever, we are all the same".

I personally believe that the only way to beat racism is "together" and that in trying to overcome it in individual groups we are doomed to failure.

What is your passion and is it going to help others?

6.   Leadership & Management

I love this subject with all my heart, it's all about people
playing their part,
many senior people will never lead, they're too selfish, and
don't have the heart.
The first ingredient that many dismiss is a need to show
empathy and care,
for some it's about me, me, me, they never tell you that they're
there.

You need to Trust, Include and Empower if you want to see,
how this drives your team to show how fantastic they can be.
Leaders must embrace and respect their team, that's where the
power sits,
But some chose to ignore this point and their business ends up
in bits.

I've seen at first-hand a leader who doesn't listen or provide
backing,
he's always right, knows everybody's job and thinks his team
are lacking.
The type of guy who can't move on, because he knows he
hasn't got it,
so, he'll just hang around taking all the credit, while others do
his bit.

I have been in the leadership world all my adult life and I treat positions of leadership as a gift. I have seen at first hand the damage that can be done by people that don't have the respect or indeed, tools to hold such privileged positions, and it literally ruins careers and lives.

Not everyone can lead, and it simply isn't right to place individuals into leadership roles just because of longevity or retention. Leadership can be taught, but the lessons must be learned.

Are you a leader or do you prefer to be led? Remember, leaders who offer nothing are little more than frauds.

7.   The Arboretum

The Arboretum sits in the morning sun,
remembering the things that our boys have done.
Not in a way that glorifies war, death, or pain,
but in the way that lets us remember their sacrifice again.

I see the names of many friends and very close mates,
that never came home but live on within these gates.
Young men and women who gave their all in the fight,
so others could live in a way that was right.

The beautiful sunshine burns through a brilliant blue sky,
covering this place in a blanket of comfort, and I know exactly
why.
These boys and girls have given their all, and then come home
to rest,
this Arboretum has been built on this spot to ensure they have
the best.

Home again from wherever they fell,
in a place where loved ones can come to visit and tell.
They will live forever in this beautiful garden of rest,
built in the memory and honour of the very best.

If ever a soldier says that they aren't frightened in battle, they are either idiots or simply lying. Soldiers respect life and accept that they may be called upon to make the ultimate sacrifice, but that is very different.

If the worst should happen, there is no doubt that these brave men and women would want to be brought home. To understand this, take a walk in our National Memorial Arboretum.

Where is your special place and what does it mean to you?

8.   Why The Good Guys?

It's always the good that die young we all say,
but it just isn't right that it's so often that way.
Genuine, decent and honest folk, with the ladder of life to
climb,
taken too early for being in the wrong place at the wrong time.

Maybe it's because God needs his best angels to help do good,
none of us know but we will always wonder why he would.
Take those he has given us and claim them back early this way,
because we loved them and wanted them all to stay.

When loved ones pass too early there is enormous pain,
you'd give anything you have to bring them back again.
But life must go on, no matter how hard it may be,
that's what our loved ones would say, there's no other option
you see.

Nobody knows how long they will be here, and we must all be
clear,
to show the love, compassion, and care for those we hold so
very dear.
Whilst their parting is fraught with pain, please don't despair,
I know from personal experience, if you need them, they'll be
there.

*We all know the saying "Only the good die young" and
thankfully most of us are never touched by it directly. During
my service I was forced to recall this saying on several
occasions; sadly, it is only too accurate.*

*I have seen the worst that man can do to man, and each time it
involved a decent, caring human being trying to do their best.
A father, mother, son, or daughter taken way too early.*

9.   Stay Out of The Crowd

We've been in lockdown for a long time now,
showing care for others and agreeing how,
we could pull together for everyone's sake,
doing all we were asked for the difference it could make.

It's a long time since we've put others first,
Where we've shown our hearts and a massive thirst.
To do the right thing, keep us all safe and sound,
I was proud to be British keeping our feet on the ground.

But just as we are making the progress we need,
we stop helping ourselves and pay no heed.
Thousands go out because they have seen the sun,
Reverting to type showing care for nobody, nor the harm
they've done.

Have we forgotten so quickly and become so callous,
that we do stupid things that show such malice.
We all should fear a second wave and now it's more likely in
time,
So, think about your actions or more will die in their prime.

We fought hard to win the battle and the war was within reach,
sadly, we got cocky thinking it won't get me, and headed to the
beach.
When this all started, we showed true British spirit, real grit,
but COVID's still here so follow the rules or more will surely
be hit.

For those who disregard the rules and believe their actions fair,
how will you react when your loved ones are hit, will you
suddenly care?
Will you feel the same as the day you joined the madding
crowd,
Or will your heart be broken because of loss; will that make you
proud?

This tells the story of our struggle to maintain the amazing societal discipline that we showed at the start of the COVID 19 pandemic. As a nation we demonstrated the British stiff upper lip at the outset, and amazingly, the vast majority of people played by the rules; my surprise was simply because it had been a very long time since we had been called upon to behave in such a subservient manner. Our care for our neighbours shone through and we did it!

As the months dragged on and key lessons from our leadership fell way below the expected standards, we understandably started to lose our discipline. Fed up and hurt, some were tempted to throw caution to the wind, so when the sun started to show its face, we headed for the beaches in numbers. Letting our guard down too early set us back and sadly cost some additional lives. I know many will regret such actions.

10. Shirt & Tie

I joined the British Army when I was just a boy,
I'd never worn a tie before unless it was a toy.
You need to be smart if you want to gain respect,
That was the message that I was given, and it was pretty direct.

So, I learned to do a half Windsor, and a full one too,
and when I did my tie up, I was always smarter than you.
All through my service I tied a wicked knot and could do it in
the dark,
Not sure why I needed to though, we had light, and it was never
that stark.

On entering the world of business, it helped my case,
I wore a good suit, a shirt and tie and made it across first base.
I never fully understood why so many guys wore an old, frayed
suit,
in my world if your suit was crap you usually got the boot.

*To take pride in your appearance is a good thing, and it
demonstrates a level of respect that is too often cast aside in the
modern world.*

*It isn't always necessary and, in many instances, it's totally
unsuitable, but in certain circumstances it is entirely
appropriate; let's be honest, does a PM without a tie carry the
same authority for most of us?*

11. Why Support a Buffoon

The most powerful country in the world is run by a total buffoon,
if that doesn't concern you, you must be as much of a loon.
Just think whose finger hovers over that button every single day,
if that doesn't cause sleepless nights, your head is facing the wrong way.

Donald doesn't listen whatever his people, or America might say,
If that doesn't worry you, then you already know, it's his way or the highway.
The President decided that COVID wasn't a threat, and he told the nation so,
if that doesn't scare you then the truth should, it's here and it just won't go.

Mr Trump throws things out there without the slightest thought,
if that doesn't annoy you, I'm amazed because it makes me fraught.
Another 5 years of this madness, the hatred, and the pain,
if that doesn't terrify America, we'll just have it all again.

When Donald Trump was elected President of the world's most powerful nation, I felt a blast of real despair. The man was a known misogynist, a bully, and total buffoon. As they say, only in America!

However, this guy would have his finger on the nuclear button and was therefore, in a position where he could literally wipe nations of the face of the earth. I can genuinely say that thought did not sit easily with me!

12. 40 Years

Next year sees our 40th year together, through thick and thin,
I wouldn't want it any other way, that's the relationship we're in.
I've had a wonderful happy life, we do everything together,
I knew I'd got the right girl back then and that we'd be forever.

We have lived in so many places, it was great fun at the time,
but now we're settled in Wiltshire, just as we enter our prime.
We lived in ten houses over 19 years, without stability or roots,
so having been here 20 years, you could say we have filled our boots.

Holidays in Hawaii, Bahamas and around the globe we went,
we're happiest at home now, the best times we have spent.
Our lives will change as we grow old, but in a very good way,
we can spend more time together, each and every day.

We are a small family but we're very happy you know,
we enjoy life, have no worries and lots of places to go.
Whatever the future holds, we'll deal with it I'll bet,
that's how we have done things, since the very first day we met.

*I have been completely in love with my wife since the day we
met and to reach 40 years together was a milestone for which I
was truly grateful. Now, as the years go by my greatest wish is
that God will grant us many more years together; nothing else
matters.*

13. America's Missing the Point

The world's most powerful nation has got itself in a mess,
with a leader who has no clue or care, it's something they must
redress.
Brash and loud they have always been, but they have done a lot
of good,
the world needs America to stop wars, not start them, providing
care and food.

The rednecks back Trump, they don't care what he says,
he likes and supports guns; he's very set in his ways.
Normal people are horrified by the things that he does,
it doesn't bother Donald; it seems to give him a buzz.

America must wake up and consider their global role,
Or the world could find itself in a terrible black hole.
The Russians, the Chinese, the North Koreans too,
Could take a very different approach to what's good for me and
you.

*As the Trump era unfolded, I got increasingly concerned that
having made a terrible mistake, the American people seemed to
be powerless to stop the bandwagon.*

*Biden was a poor choice as a challenger and although he is a
much more balanced leader, he was simply past his best as a
statesman. This situation scared me and the Trump mob that
attacked the Capitol Building was terrifying; the world averted
disaster by a whisker when Joe Biden won.*

14. BLM

Black Lives Matter, just as much as all the rest,
but All Lives Matter don't they, surely that would be the best.
There really isn't a difference, we are all exactly the same,
If you cut us, we bleed, shoot us we die, this isn't some kind of game.

Why do we need to worry about the colour of our skin?
it causes so much hatred, and nobody will win.
We are all the same on the inside, a lovely shade of pink,
so, who gives a damn about the outside, we've found the common link.

Blood is red whether you're black or white, so let's not let it spill,
we all need that blood to stay alive, and it's not right to kill.
Why don't we all forget about this stupid pointless fight?
put an arm around each other and try to make it right.

Our ancestors made big mistakes so many years ago,
but we couldn't stop them, we weren't around you know.
There can never be an excuse, to treat fellow humans this way,
I have never done so, nor have most people around today.

I don't even like to hear the word "hate", it is corrosive and deadly; the only context in which I would ever use it is against racism. If I could achieve one thing in life, it would be to overcome racism in its entirety.

*We are all the same, the same colour inside and when we bleed. Every life has the same value, but we can only overcome this nightmare together, so let's all accept that fact **AND GET IT DONE**.*

15. When I Was In School

I loved to write stories when I was just a wee boy,
I had more fun doing with that than with any kind of toy.
Whether it was monsters, or silly old giants I didn't really care,
I'd just close my eyes and think for a bit and get transported there.

Old Molly Williamson used to push me on, and she would often say,
keep telling stories you're good at it, you'll be an author one day.
I didn't really listen to her and that's a shame you know,
because I think she may be right and into that author I'll grow.

She's probably long gone by now, sitting up there in the sky,
I wish that I had listened to her, rather than keep on asking why.
I've always loved words and telling stories, I've done it all my life, is that what Molly was telling me, to save me some trouble and strife.

The power of words is incredible and can help overcome most things; if we are sad just listening to a story can change that, make us laugh, smile, and feel better.

Mankind has been built on stories and we must never lose that art.

16. Don't You Love a Dialect?

My pride in being British is very strong you know,
I love hearing different accents everywhere I go.
In the far north of Scotland their speech is very clear,
most folk don't realise; they speak Queen's English here.

If you come down the country just a little bit,
you'll hit the Doric speakers and you'll get none of it.
Travel a bit further south and then you will hit Dundee,
stay there just a little while and you'll understand a bit, just you
wait and see.

When you come down to Glasgow with Edinburgh off to the
east,
you'll be ok in Edinburgh, but the Glaswegian accent's a beast.
Don't worry too much though there's plenty more to go,
the next stop would be the Toon, now that will be a show.

In Yorkshire there will be a challenge, as every Riding has its
way,
what you might hear in Harrogate, in Sheffield holds no sway.
It gets more challenging when you head out to the west,
Mancs have a slow and steady drone, but Scouse is more
cryptic than the rest.

The Brummie twang will fox you when you arrive there too,
they say things like "am ye" and "y'am" and that will be
strange to you.
Across to the west you could hit Stoke and they'll have
something to say,
there aren't too many miles between them, but they talk in a
different way.

When you get down to the southern belt then it gets really great,
in London they have cockney's who make up their own slang at
a rate.
Whilst in Bristol they are west-country and everything's gurt
lush,
if you come from the Home Counties, then that's just verbal
mush.

I mustn't forget Wales of course, in the north they sound like a
Scouse,
in the valley's it's simply not the same, it's a very different
house;
They all speak some Wenglish but very few speak Welsh,
They are just as confused by it as everybody else.

If you nip across the water, then your problems will really start,
the Irish lilt is soft with a lovely twang, but in North you'll
simply lose heart.
So that's my tour of the British Isles, our language is complex,
not easy,
foreign folk find it tough, they think we're all the same, but
that's a little cheesy.

*Our country has more dialects than most and to be honest, for
such a small set of islands, this diversity sets us apart. I love
the fact that using your forefinger and little finger as a measure
against a large-scale map, you can step from south to north,
east to west, and find a different dialect at every
point.*

*This is a key component of the character of our country and
whilst we should be proud of the rich and diverse range of
people living here, we must also work to protect and retain this
character. The UK just wouldn't be the same without our
dialects!*

17. I Love my Merc

When I was a kid, I loved my toys and especially the cars,
but I never thought I'd own a Merc, that's reaching for the stars.
My first car was a banger, it didn't even have a key,
I just crossed the wires, and it would start, that was enough for
me.

As the years went past, I'd upgrade my car and bring some
comfort in,
a radio or a tape deck made a difference and were what I would
call a win.
Then came the luxury years where my cars got big and flash,
full of amazing tech with anything you wanted if you had the
cash.

Now we have come to the important point where we can all
help out,
to get rid of fossil fuels that damage our world and turn things
about.
I have driven a range of hybrid cars and that makes me feel
good,
now I have actually got my Merc, the next step is full electric if
I could.

*When I was growing up, it was very unusual for people to buy
and own a new car. Their pride and joy would inevitably be a
highly polished but beaten-up banger. Applying the elbow
grease to make it look its best was never a problem, we all liked
nice things, right?*

*It seems so much has changed in this world, where second hand
just isn't enough, and everything must be shiny and new.
Personally, I think if it was you that applied that shine, using
your elbow grease, the shine is just a little deeper.*

18. Are We Still British?

Are we still British I would ask, if I could speak to Tony Blair,
he tore up our Union and threw bits of it everywhere.
I'm a Highland Scot but British too, I'm proud of our Union
flag,
but Mr Blair and his cronies have cost us dear, and it was all a
blag.

Devolved government within a union, is that the way to go?
it isn't very British and that's the trouble you know.
Decisions can be difficult but with one voice for all,
we can make them quickly and not wait for the country to stall.

It's too late now to turn things back, where it becomes a single
load,
that's a real sadness for me, it drives us apart and takes us down
the wrong road.
I don't think it helps us as a people, when it's plain to for all to
see,
that we are four little countries now and not the power we used
to be.

*Being a Highland Scot is hugely important to me; my blood is
Scottish, and my heart will always lie there. <u>BUT</u> I am British
through and through.*

*Together we have made this United Kingdom one of the
greatest nations on Earth: whilst we have made mistakes, we
have done far more good than bad. We have stood up to
tyrants, mass murderers, and despots around the world,
delivering safety and sanctuary to millions. We have learned
from our mistakes, so let's celebrate our successes. Britain is
Great!*

19. Donald's Tweets

His tweets are often silly and can be made in very bad taste,
the misuse of a platform for change, isn't that a terrible waste.
The President of America should not be doing that, I can hear most people say,
if he stopped to consider the things he says, then some might go away.

I don't think he's terribly bright, or maybe he just doesn't care or regret,
he'll be ok and still have it all, while the rest of us face the threat.
Whether he's a racist I don't think we know, maybe we never will,
I just cringe when he speaks and worry about the blood he could so easily spill.

Come on Mr President, it's not all about you and others have rights you know,
there are decent people all over the world that believe it's your time to go.
If you should win another term, please show you can learn from the past,
where you have made mistakes, got things wrong but that doesn't have to last.

You are probably starting to think I have a vendetta against Mr Trump, I don't, but neither do I believe it is right for somebody of his racist, sexist, and limited intellect to run the world's richest economy.

America must remain a force for good, a nation committed to playing a leading part in world politics. Mr Trump was unsuited to that critical role, and he must never be allowed to hold this office again, for all our sakes.

20. Guns

Why does anybody need a gun in this day and age, any threat can be overcome,
by people we entrust to keep us safe, and we know where they come from.
So, legislation shouldn't exist just to let folks get their own way,
if you don't have a need or it's not part of your job, let's take them all away.

Too many people have lost their lives and we must ask just why,
guns still exist within your culture, with the result that people die.
Even little children aren't safe in a small country town,
evil killers can visit them and simply shoot them down.

So many innocents die in the US, every single year,
we must make our stand, remove the guns before it happens here.
Our police don't want to carry guns, but we're forcing them down that way,
if we don't sort things out pretty quick, it will be standard practice I'd say.

I have fought alongside our American allies and have been very thankful for their incredible firepower. However, the tragedies that unfold almost daily in the US are completely unacceptable. People, many of them children, are dying unnecessarily because of the antiquated gun laws.

The second amendment, which gives the right to bear arms was historically necessary 200 years ago, to protect life. It has no place in a modern society and the US Government needs to repeal it. Surely the leaders of the Free World have the courage and commitment to stop these horrific murder sprees.

21. Head or Heart

When you know it's time you left a job, because it's not right
for you,
you have to go with your head and do what it says to do.
Don't hide behind the money or compromise your ways,
if you do, you'll regret it for the remainder of your days.

People make a business and true leaders know that's true,
it makes it hard to step away, but you must do what's right for
you.
Good folk would never criticise that choice, they usually
respect you more,
for standing up for what is right and walking out that door.

Now is the time to give your heart a say,
what is it you want to do because there's always a way.
There will be something in your heart that has long been a
dream for you,
go and get it now, it's your chance to make it real and truly
enjoy what you do.

Life is too short and precious to let it slip on past,
take a grip, do what you want, and your happiness will last.
There may be risks along the way that you will need to face,
but they're your risks that you're taking, not theirs in any case.

*This is my way of saying consider what's best for you when
making key life choices. It's very easy to chase the money and
to believe it will deliver happiness; it seldom does.*

*Always consider what matters most in your life, family, health,
wellbeing, work/life balance all play their part. The one thing
we can't do is turn back time, so use it wisely.*

22. Time for a Puppy

Every night when I got home, I knew he would be there,
sitting waiting, he just wouldn't go anywhere.
How he knew when I'd get home, is anybody's guess,
but he never missed the opening door and I thought oh, god
bless.

When they go to doggy heaven up there in the sky,
it often takes a very long time before you can say goodbye.
For me it took a lot of years before I could let it go,
I missed him more than I can say, and it made me feel quite
low.

I don't want to replace him, that wouldn't work anyway,
but it's time for a new cold nose to greet me when I come home
and say,
Hello pup I've missed you, it's been a long hard day,
then you feel that loyalty and love in every single way.

*I have always been an animal lover, and particularly of dogs. I
hated the quarantine system when living abroad, which meant
your pets had to be subjected to six months in kennels before
being allowed back into the country.*

*So, I waited until we were settled back in UK before we got our
black Labrador, Benjy. I loved him from the moment I saw him
hiding behind a tree as a pup and we became inseparable. I
lost him when he was 16 years old, and it has taken me 14 years
to get to a point where I can think about another dog.*

23. Suicide

Suicide is something you can never work out, why did they want to go,
families rack their brains, but the truth is, they will simply never know.
The hurt and pain never leaves and nor does racking your brain,
you need to understand so you go over it, time and time again.

I'm pretty sure that there was no intent to hurt us, or to let us down,
they were just unhappy and didn't wish to wear a frown.
Nobody knows what another thinks, or how much hurt they know,
rather than share their pain with us they may think it's better to go.

This choice is often made with no recourse to others, there are no signs,
they just want the pain to end, to stop the hurt within their minds.
It doesn't mean they don't still hold you in their heart and love you like before,
in their mind they don't want you to suffer, that's why they step through the door.

Nobody knows what is running through another person's mind, nor the depth of despair they may have sunk to. All we can do is try to always be there, ready to listen.

The feeling of pain and personal failure when the signs are missed is indescribable, but please don't attribute blame; that person didn't love you any less, it was their own pain they were addressing. Remember them for who they were. Always.

24. Fergie Was Ours

I support my hometown club, we used to be something special you know,
think back to Gothenburg in 83 and we all thought, just watch our Fergie go.
The bad thing is he did just that 3 short years later, and we felt real pain,
he headed off to Manchester, would we ever win again.

The first years at United didn't go his way, they lost quite a few,
so, we were sitting in Aberdeen thinking you got what's coming to you.
But he's a genius as everybody said, he'll eventually come good,
in 86 he did just that, the FA Cup above his head he knew just where he stood.

He's no flash in the pan our Alex, he's a true legend now you know,
I only wish it could have been with us and he didn't have to go.
He was still in red in any case, so that made it easier to take,
but it was with United not the Dons that every record he would break.

Fergie is retired now, racing horses, and drinking fine wine,
we knew he would be a legend, he got everything over the line.
He's a knight of the realm, a Scottish Sir with a very bright red nose,
we should all hail Fergie and hope it's some time until he goes.

I love football and have always believed it is a force for good. It's our national sport and we shared it with the world, what a gift. I personally think that football fans should support their local team, not teams from a different town, city, or region. The local club is part of the areas identity and as such, it should be a source of pride.

It is hard not to wonder why people choose to support a team from a place with which they have no ties, or is it simply glory hunting?

25. I'm Not Old

I don't understand why people have a thing about growing old,
life definitely gets better with age, a time for us all to be bold.
We gain more knowledge, understand our limits, and make
better decisions too,
we don't make the same mistake as much as we used to do.

I have seen many folk that let themselves grow old, bent and
stooping down,
I really don't get it and wonder if they're simply behaving like a
clown.
Stay young in the mind and young at heart, it will help you keep
control,
of an ageing process that some just accept, and let it go on a
roll.

I'm planning to give old a miss and to just keep pushing on,
if that doesn't work, it was worth a try, and I'll keep it up until
the day I'm gone.
Life is very precious, and you should take every chance you get,
to live it to the full and avoid all types of regret.

*It makes me sad to see people behaving as if they are old, just
because they hit a certain age. It's as if getting to a certain
point in life means that we should stop enjoying ourselves, why?*

*Age is no more than a number and if you are fit and healthy,
enjoy it for as long as is possible. It's a fantastic feeling to
realise that your experience and knowledge can be shared to
help others. Don't overlook your chance to do good things,
help others, and make a difference. That's what life is all about
and it's fun.*

26. Clean Shoes

I walk into a room and the interview starts, I want to see them succeed,
but I can't avoid what matters to me, their shoes are very dirty indeed.
What does that say about the interviewee, the person in that chair?
a good suit, a shirt and tie but do the shoes show they don't really care.

Preparation is everything, that's what people say,
so how come his shoes aren't clean, is it different his way.
He answers questions in a good strong voice, confident as we can see,
maybe he only prepares for what he thinks will be important to me.

I guess the key point here, is that our futures are often held in another's hand, there is only so much we can do, but if we lack concentration where do we stand? It's not just shoes you know, its first impressions I'm on about, take your time to make sure you prepare, don't let it catch you out.

Having pride in your appearance is a good trait and tells a lot about a person's character. When you have very little, it teaches you to respect what you do have, to take care of it, and to maintain it.

Shoes are a perfect example, where a little bit of polish and effort can make even a tired, worn pair look much better than they are. Why do some people frown on personal pride, is it just laziness?

27. It's A Beautiful World

The world is such a beautiful place, but sometimes we do forget,
we don't really take care of it; that's something we may regret.
If we don't start to change and show it the respect it deserves,
there won't be a world to live in and we don't have any reserves.

If you are lucky and get the chance to travel far,
you'll see things that will amaze you and often it's where they are.
I have walked a lot of beaches in places that could stop your heart,
whether it was in Hawaii, Barbados, or the island of St Bart.

The thing that strikes a chord with me, is the fact you don't need to go far,
our little islands have everything, but we forget how beautiful they are.
Don't take our world for granted, we need to keep it safe for all,
If we don't, we'll just destroy it, we'll be heading for a fall.

The beauty of our planet is truly breath-taking, whether its snow-capped mountains, the ocean, forests, or even desert. We really need to take greater care of it, or we will eventually destroy it.

This is not a scare mongering statement, but a simple fact. We are all responsible and must act now! We owe it to each other, to our children and to our grandchildren.

28. What Does Family Mean?

Family to me is a conundrum, I really don't think it should be,
it should be really easy, for all your family to see.
We need to look after each other and provide love and care,
but since I left home many years ago, my brothers have not
been there.

I'd struggle across a continent to visit my family at home,
they wouldn't travel but a few miles, it was always me that had
to roam.
No invitation to family events and I couldn't help wondering
why,
I'd only ever been kind to them, yet they treated me like this, it
often raised a sigh.

It didn't matter though, I had my mum and my little sister to
see,
if my brothers couldn't be bothered it was sad, but I didn't let it
hurt me.
I have spent a lot of time wondering if it was my fault in some
way,
but I've never done anything, nothing to push them away.

My own little family is happy, we're content and real,
we are really close, support each other, just how a family should
feel.
I'm sorry I have lost my brothers but maybe I worry too much,
but after 47 years it's probably too late, they'll never get in
touch.

Family used to mean so much more to society, and perhaps the breakdown of the family unit is at the heart of many societal issues. In the UK the multi-generational family home is a thing of the past; most of our younger generation have never experienced it.

The curse of care homes has been upon us for many years, and the COVID period has exposed the cruelty behind it, with older family members dying alone. Many lives are shortened by entry to a care facility, whereas being with family can have the opposite effect. Is it too late to embrace the family once again?

29. What Do People Need?

People have a range of complex needs and sometimes I just
wonder why,
surely a roof over your head and food on the table is enough for
any guy.
Stepping beyond that it's about health and happiness in my
view,
if you have all these things, then you should be grateful too.

People need money to live their life and I accept that's true,
but do they really need more than everyone else, more than me
or you.
Greed is ugly and has no place in our world or our souls,
people who ignore this fact often end up in very dark deep
holes.

Family, health, food, and drink, that's all we really require,
we don't need too many other things, just to control our desire.
We often think we need things, but it often isn't true,
all we need are the simple things that matter to me and you.

*There is an argument that we all have and expect too much. My
parents had a golden rule: if you can't afford it, you can't have
it! It guarded against debt, encouraged saving, and made the
wait worthwhile.*

*In today's world, it's a case of why wait when I can get it on
credit, whether it is affordable doesn't come into it. Does this
deliver happiness or despair. What do you think?*

30. My Family's 100ᵗʰ Birthday

I thank the Lord every single day,
that I found the Royal Signals along my way.
I owe my Corps a debt that can never be repaid,
that's the debt of gratitude for every dream they made.
My friends have got my back, whether I'm in or out,
that's something very special for me, that I can shout about.
This family of ours is very special, some would say unique,
it's the type of thing money can't buy, but all good people seek.
To all fellow Scaley's I know that you'll attest,
we love the Royal Corps of Signals, it's simply the best.

Certa Cito

I have tried to explain the "military family" mentality to many people over the years, but it is something truly unique. Where else in life do you routinely come across people that you haven't seen in 20-30 years and a bond immediately exists.

*It may happen in individual friendships, but never as the default in any other walk of life and that is **special**. This is a club where lifetime membership cannot be bought.*

31. So What's Next?

COVID gives us a lot to think about in the coming years,
it will take some time, but we will relax our fears.
We need to be sensible, and not lose our head,
So many have been taken, we have too many dead.

Our attitude and care for each other is key,
if we take too many risks, we will never be free.
Most people care enough to be safe and protect other folk,
it's those that don't that scare me, those who think it's a joke.

But let's be clear, we must strive to stay,
at a distance from each other, each and every day.
We can still meet and talk, but social distancing is a must,
we will only stay safe, if we show respect and some trust.

When we go to the pub, or have some food to eat,
we will need to be careful; it won't be a normal meet and greet.
No handshakes or kissing twice on the cheek,
just touch elbows, I know, it's a bit meek.

Think of the staff that will look after us all, in every way,
they don't want to catch the virus, but they're at risk every day.
Respect each other and show common sense,
as you sit in a booth with what looks like a fence.

For 5 long months we have fought this killer disease and yet,
we have nothing to show for it, but it hasn't won, and it won't I
bet.
Humans are strongest with their backs against the wall,
so do your worst COVID, we're not going to fall.

The human spirit is truly remarkable and that was demonstrated so often during COVID Lockdown. People refused to be broken by this terrible disease, businesses did not give up, and despite terrible loss, we made it out the other side.

Those that were lost will never be forgotten and we know that it hasn't gone away, but we will learn to live with it. Mankind's strength and tenacity in times of hardship often bring out the very best in human nature, where our true care and love for each other always shines through.

32.   Entering The Twilight Years

As you get older and the years slip past,
it is easy to panic and think it's going too fast.
But just stand back and take a nice deep breath,
the future's in your hands, don't just sit there waiting for death.

There is so much to do in this wonderful place,
don't amble around with a frown on your face.
Get stuck in and control your own fate,
if you do, you'll realise that life is still great.

Growing old is a pleasure that many don't get,
so let's be thankful that you've had a let.
Enjoy it, have fun and show everybody out there,
you're not scared, you know just how to care.

As a youngster I remember people aged fifty or more,
acting like they were ancient, and always very sore.
Now things have changed, and I am pleased to say,
fifty is no age, the way we live today.

I've been twenty-one for forty years and I've enjoyed them all,
I'm hoping for many, many more, before I take the fall.
I'll probably get rumbled and have to admit,
I'm in my sixties now, but I'm still pretty fit.

Life is what you make it and that's a simple fact,
but you don't have to be old, if it's just an act;
Whilst the lord still provides me with all that I need,
I'm going to enjoy life that's my way indeed.

Getting old can be so much fun; it never fails to amaze me how I enjoy each decade that little bit more. Maybe it's because I feel I have more to offer, or maybe because I'm still here!

Life is a gift and very precious, so enjoy it, many never get that chance. When things seem bad or you're feeling down, just remember how lucky you are to live in this beautiful world of ours. Things are never as bad as they might appear.

33. The Heroes I've Known

When we consider the people we've known,
we never think of heroes because they're our own.
But as I sit here and look back on the life I've led,
I have known heroes, they're in my heart and my head.

Back in 82 I lost several great friends, they were just young
boys,
doing their best to gain freedom, but of course guns aren't toys.
Lost in a war fought far, far away, they never came home,
but they will never be forgotten because they're our own.

That was a bad decade for me, later terrorists took another
three,
just a young boy only 22, bludgeoned for being where he
shouldn't be.
Two other real friends who didn't deserve what they got,
posing no threat but still both were shot.

These guys were heroes, of that I have no doubt,
but they were also the friends that I often think about.
Where would life have taken them, what might they have done?
nobody knows we can only dream, they're not here, they're
gone.

My life is much richer for meeting each of these lads, yes it
makes me sad,
I remember them every day, some of the best mates I've ever
had.
Each has left a legacy, in a range of different ways,
I'll proudly carry them with me, for the rest of my days.

Hero is a word that is overused, but I have had the privilege of meeting a few in my life. The one common denominator is this: they put others first. It's very special thing to do and doesn't have to cost a life; in most cases it doesn't cost a thing.

34.   Life's Lessons

As we travel through life, we learn something new every day,
let's channel these lessons in the most positive way.
To help each other be the best we can be, the very best versions
of you and me,
working together will make us all stronger, give it a try and
you'll see.

We all know someone who is struggling and finding life tough,
so, let's pull together, help them climb out of the rough.
To care for others is a very special trait, it shows our true face,
as decent people, who are genuine members of the human race.

When life is good and treating us well, we should share our
happiness and joy,
with those less blessed, who have nothing to show, but we are
often coy.
To share with others should be our aim, because in life that's
part of the game,
it's not just about us, it's about being fair and offering others
the same.

It really doesn't take much to consider others and how we can
assist,
to make their lives better, provide love and support to help them
persist.
To be there and listen to their trials and their pain,
will help them to move forward and to live again.

This poem is just about being kind and doing good things. The next time you walk past somebody down on their luck, just remember, "there but for the grace of God go I".

It is truly amazing how good it feels to give somebody that is hungry some food, or to speak to them like they mean something. Put yourself in their shoes.

35. Smart or Not?

I've always been frustrated by those who try to show,
that introducing complexity is the only way to go.
It's usually rooted in their need to feel superior, that only they
can find a way,
but the truth is very different, that's what I would always say.

If simple will work, then you should strive to make it so,
it's about finding an answer, finding the right way to go.
Simple is as simple does, it's a well-worn ditty, championed by
those who think it's all very witty,
but keeping it simple will work for most, even for those who
inevitably get shitty.

If your driver is to demonstrate your brighter than most,
it often works out that it's little more than a silly boast.
Increasing time, effort and inevitably cost,
by the time you've delivered, the need has been lost.

Think about what's right, what will get the job done,
not how difficult you can make it, because you think you're the
one.
It's about finding an answer, a solution that works, not focusing
on greed,
effective, efficient, and affordable too, delivering quickly to
meet the need.

*Life would be so much easier if we did the simple things more
readily. I have often wondered what drives some folk to seek
the more difficult option in so many instances and can only
surmise it as being for their own gratification.*

No, it doesn't make sense to me either.

36. Giving Back

We have all got something to give back, to help others make their way,
through the challenges that we all meet, as we travel through life each day.
It will make you feel better, to give something to those who truly need,
to receive a little comfort, care and help, so they themselves succeed.

One of the gifts in life is the chance to share,
to show strangers love and to show them you care.
Don't walk on by when someone's in trouble, step in and help them out,
showing compassion and love for others, surely that's what life's about.

While many will make their way through life without any distress,
please think of others, with no family, home, or whose life is just a mess.
It's often the result of something, over which they have no control,
they usually don't choose this life, it's not just the way they roll.

There is little more rewarding, than helping rebuild a life,
to give somebody that bit of support to overcome their strife.
Please don't consider them useless, stupid or even worse,
they are people, their lives matter, helping others is privilege, not a curse.

I personally believe that we all have something to give and there are certainly plenty in need. Providing that bit of help can make a huge difference to the life of those less fortunate and let's be honest, most of us have more than we need.

Sharing is therapeutic, try it.

37.   No Regrets

I never do regrets, they simply don't work, or add any value to you,
that way I focus on the happy, positive things in my life, as I always try to do.
We never try to get things wrong, it just occasionally doesn't work out,
so don't entertain any negative thought, just try harder next time I shout.

Many things are needed to make life successful, rewarding and fun,
positivity is certainly one such gift, whilst happiness is yet another one.
Being kind and considerate of others, will go a very long way,
to building relationships and friendships, that will mature and stay.

I learned very early to value people, our number one resource,
to show empathy and respect is essential, and very powerful of course.
Treat folk in a way that shows you have a heart, and that you listen too,
that way they know you care and will put their trust in you.

Leaders and managers play a critical role, but they are not the same,
leadership and management go hand in glove, but they're from a separate game.
In that place it's all about the team, in which there is no "I",
if we remember that point we will get things right, we will always get by.

We all make mistakes because we are human, but it's what we do to overcome these errors that really matters. Nobody makes mistakes deliberately, so rather than pore over them, let's learn from them; therein lies improvement.

The team is what truly makes things work, always take them with you. Always remember, "There is no I in team".

38. Don't Let Diabetes Win

When I was told I was diabetic, I didn't worry too much,
it's just a bit of a nuisance I thought, it's not dangerous as such.
Now that's a mistake I will always regret, and don't want others to make,
because if you don't respect it, it will eat you up and plan your life to take.

It's a silent attacker who won't be in a rush to win, adding misery is its way,
but it never gives up as the years go by, it knows most will allow it to stay.
This is a fight that very few win, we like our food and sugar too much,
that works for diabetes, it uses it as its crutch.

But there are simple ways to hit back, because you need to fight,
if you don't it will get you, and that just isn't right.
Find a bit of time for fitness, it doesn't like that,
it prefers it if we're lazy, and even more if we're a little bit fat.

We all have weaknesses that play right into its hands,
mine was chocolate, sweets and biscuits, nothing overly grand.
But that was enough to let diabetes win, it attacked whenever it could,
trying to take my limbs, my eyes or anything from where I stood.

I let it win for far too long, I was always too busy to do the things it hates,
like visit the Gym, eat at the right time, or listen to advice from mates.
But things have changed Mr Diabetes, I'm up for the fight, you'll see,
you've never seen my stronger side, I won't let you beat me.

I'm going to fly the flag and build an army to kick your butt,
to show everyone that you're a coward, with no fight in your
gut.
We'll stop the one-sided sneaky approach, that doesn't get our
attention,
and together we will beat you, through strength, awareness and
prevention.

*I have been a diabetic for over 20 years and hate the disease
with a passion. I call it the silent killer because it creeps up on
you, exploiting your weaknesses, too much sugar, too many
biscuits, or not enough physical exercise. The point, of course,
is it can be avoided if we are careful.*

*It's not, as many believe, an issue for fat folk, it can get the
skinny one's too If they chose to ignore the threat. I want to
fight it with all I have got and want you all to join that fight.
Let's beat diabetes together.*

39.   Life is so Special

Life is so very special, you must never take it for granted,
because it can be gone in the blink of an eye, before it has even
started.
I love everything about my life and live every day as if it's my
last,
because one day it will be, so I look to the future not the past.

I often think "How lucky am I", just why is my life so blessed,
I don't know whether I deserve it, maybe I'm just luckier than
the rest.
But I will never take it for granted, that would simply be wrong,
for too many others have nothing, their lives aren't stable or
strong.

I grew up in the Highlands, where kids run happy and free,
unlike so many in cities, where they are lucky just to see a tree.
As a young boy I joined the Army, where I was tutored and
taught the right way,
to have standards, integrity and care for others, each and every
day.

"There's no I in team" was a favourite quip, but I knew it was
great advice,
those who don't understand that point, are usually not very nice.
Everybody matters and we were always taught, to never leave a
man behind,
but that is often forgotten in this cruel world, as many of you
will find.

There can be very little between life and death, sometimes just a blink of the eye. When you have seen life taken this way, it will never leave you.

Live your life to the fullest and for everyone you have lost along the way, if you don't, it's your fault, there's nobody else to blame.

40.   Satchmo Said...

It can be funny what sticks in your mind, simple throw away lines that lie,
whirring around in your head, even when you don't know why.
Sometimes they are lessons that keep you safe, reminding you not to do,
silly, lazy or dangerous things that could be bad for you.

Why do some folk have a knack of saying stuff that makes you think?
while others make a lot of noise, which you forget it in a blink.
Is it the good guys, the strong guys or just those you respect and trust?
that leave their mark upon you, their advice becoming a must.

Many things have stuck with me, as the years have rolled on past,
I try to listen and make use of clever points, the ones I think will last.
But as you get older the points may not linger, they simply slip away,
so when the time comes that you need them, you memory may stray.

There is one line that I hope I will never forget, I call it the key to life,
it's a line from a song and it says it all, I often repeat it to my wife.
Satchmo said, "it's a wonderful life but what you make of it is up to you",
it's so very important that we remember it because it's absolutely true.

Louis Armstrong, a black American cornetist, was a real character and had many things to say. This line has always stuck with me and reminds me that your life is in your own hands so make the best of it.

With a voice like Louis, I think he definitely did.

41. Mother's Day

If I could travel up to Heaven, to see Mum for just one day,
I'd take her in my arms and hold her tight, and take my time to
say;
I love you Mum and I've missed you so, my life has never been
the same,
your love and presence were always there to guide me through
life's game.

I'd pass you a bunch of roses, because it's Mother's Day today,
if I could bring you back from Heaven, I'd hand you another,
every single day.
You did so much to prepare me to become the best that I could
be,
never seeking any praise, because I'd lost my Dad you see.

My Father was my hero, tough and strong, a proper family man,
if he was stood beside me now, he'd be the first to say "you
can".
It was you that showed me how to lead my life when God called
Dad away,
he is proud of you too Mum, he just didn't get the chance to
say.

I have to let her hand go now, but I grip on as hard as I can and
sigh,
I don't want to lose you again Mum, I tell her, as a tear runs
from my eye.
Don't worry it's not forever she says, it's just till the right time
has come,
I open my eyes and my heart fills with love, happy Mother's
Day Mum.

My mum was a very humble, hardworking little lass with the heart of a lion. Widowed at 42 years of age, she put her life into raising a 9-year-old daughter and being mother to three sons.

I have always said that I learned more about life and being the best you can be from my mum, despite a lifetime in the leadership game.

42.   A Scotsman Stands a 'Top Glencoe

As a Scotsman stands above Glencoe his heart will swell with pride,
that's my country down there he thinks, forever at my side.
A Jock will always stand his ground, whether he is huge or small and light,
because in his heart he would never give up, he would always stand and fight.

It's not because he is a bully, or that he likes to brawl,
it's because his blood is Scottish, and he gives his nation his all.
When our lands were taken many moons ago, and people had to leave,
it broke a nation's heart and those that remained could only grieve.

Families torn apart and sent on boats, so very far away,
knowing that that they would never return home, even for a single day.
But their pride in being Scottish never left their heart, nor their indomitable pride,
they all knew Scotland would never leave them, it would always be at their side.

I'm proud to be a Scot and I'll carry that to my grave, I'll head home someday,
proud also to be a British soldier, but sad to spend so long away.
I've had the best of both worlds, of that I have no doubt, but now I'm home to stay,
both Scottish and British, I wouldn't have it any other way.

Glencoe is a very special place for Highland Scots, its rugged beauty is breath-taking and awe inspiring at the same time. It was fairly central in terms of the Highland clearances and so it evokes passion and pride.

My own clan, MacGregor, owned lands to the east of Glencoe, around Dalmally, in and around Glen Orchy. I have always been interested in history and particularly that of my homeland. I recommend the story of the "Children of the Mist" which is genuinely fascinating.

43.   Valhalla's Table

At the table in Valhalla many friends have taken their seat,
as I look around the faces our eyes touch and then our smiles meet.
These are the warriors with whom I have shared my life,
some got here early, taken far too soon, others are called daily it's becoming rife.

Never beaten though, these men stand tall and proud,
soldiers all, tough but caring, their heads have never bowed.
In the Corps room in Valhalla my heart bursts with pride,
to realise these are my brothers here, who are always by my side.

They say old soldiers never die, they simply fade away,
but these guy's memory will never fade, and I know that I can say,
they will walk with me forever, keep me safe and strong of heart,
when I leave for Valhalla they will meet me on the shore, never again to part

Whilst I await my time to join them, I make this promise to them all,
to live my life to the full and be the best that I can be, I will always hear their call.
In celebration of their lives until my own is done, for all they did for me,
I will walk through life with my head held high, so that they may see.
These special men live on in my heart and that will be forever,
I thank each and every one for their friendship, sacrifice, and times we had together.

Certa Cito

I have always loved the line that "old soldiers never die; they just fade away", a little morose I guess but it tickles me, nonetheless. As a storyteller, the thought of this magical place where we will all meet again, excites me.

The real central thought here is that friends and colleagues that mean so much to me, will meet again. We will always be there for each other.

44. Dai's Memory

When work gets weary and life just starts to grate,
most guys just pick up the phone to talk to their very best mate.
You laugh and you joke, and things always seem much brighter,
you relax because you know your friendship simply couldn't be
tighter.

Then you realise that life has changed forever and he's no
longer there,
it hurts like hell because that's life, it just isn't bloody fair.
There's no best mate to speak to, nobody to answer that call,
so you end up holding it all in, facing the unclimbable wall.

You can't shake the hurt although the years just keep rolling by,
you think of your best mate, and mine was and always will be
Dai.
I miss you mate, and I will always ask why it was your time to
go,
there are things I want to share with you but you're not around
to know.

David Hugh Jones 1957-2012

*Every bloke has a best mate and Dai was mine; I have never
met anybody quite like him and we gelled the minute we met
back in 1975. We were closer than brothers because we never
fell out, not even once. A light went out in my life on July 2012.*

*I am a better person for knowing Dai, but I miss his friendship
so much. We had often spoken about getting older and how we
would sit in the Pub together and tell old soldier stories. If only
he had told me how he felt. Until we meet again my friend.*

45.   For the Nurses

I have always respected our brilliant NHS, it's a part of
Britain's best,
but the Nurses are the backbone of this institution, they never
ask for rest.
It's time to stop the clapping, it's just simply not enough,
it's time to reward them from the bottom of our heart, because
of all this stuff.

I'm trying not to focus on political points, it's the people that
matter you see,
if it wasn't for these committed folk, from the shores of every
sea,
there wouldn't be enough to care for us, to look after you and
me,
so thanks for the loyalty and commitment they have shown to
us all for free.

They have stood firm putting their lives on the line, against
COVID and so much more,
that's why I love them and welcome them to our country's
shore.
So many live so far away, they seldom see their families, or get
to hug their own,
if we don't feel humbled by that then we deserve to be alone.

Let's show them how much we care for them and the whole of
our NHS,
let's do what decent folk would do and champion their success.
The Government has already kicked them in the teeth, but they
all work for us,
it's our call when the time is right, let's all get on their bus!

George Greig 15th March 2021

I have been very lucky in life and until 2021, I had never been ill really. I have all the classic Highland diseases, of course, high BP, high cholesterol, and indigestion, but that's a rite of passage where I grew up.

All of that changed in 2021, when I spent endless weeks in hospital with everything from kidney stones to sepsis. Despite their enormous load from COVID, I saw first-hand what makes our NHS so very special, the people!

46.   Poem for Emily

Kindness is the greatest gift of all and not many bring as much as you,
it means so much when you take the time to do all the things you do.
Yours is a natural care that makes the patients all feel good,
that's not always the case you know, depending on where you're stood.

Your son and daughter will be so proud of their mum and the job you do,
finding time to love and raise them, whilst caring for others is amazing too.
People like you can be hard to find, and the NHS needs lots,
so thanks for stepping up and doing your bit, not just bringing up your tots.

When things get tough and you wonder just how you will get things done,
just remember who you are, what you love, and those that have come and gone.
That's why everybody loves you Emily, it's your care for others too,
it sets you apart from many, who don't have the caring heart you do.

Never doubt that you are valued, by those you look after every day,
or that you're loved and cherished by your kids in a very special way.
Because they only have one mum, who wiped their tears away,
for that and all you've done throughout their lives, their love grows every day.

Emily was one of the nurses that looked after me so well in hospital. She is a young single mother, working all the hours she possibly could to provide for her children. Yet she arrived at work every day with a smile on her face and put in very long shifts for very little money.

Sometimes the younger generation get a bad press, but to me Emily was an inspirational character, great mother, and a very capable health professional. In short, she would be a good role model for anybody.

47. Who'd be a Bobby?

They do a job to protect us all, but some just want to see them fall,
attacked, spat at and threatened with fire, they have to take it all.
But they are sons, daughters, mums and dads, with families just like us,
why do they do a job that puts them in harm's way, to end up under the bus?

Cops do this job to make the public safe, they are here to serve us all,
so why do some try to make their life so tough, using violence to make them fall.
These public servants are simply doing their job, putting the citizen first,
they are doing their duty, delivering their role, helping overcome the worst.

Their families standby, as their loved one's step-in harm's way,
doing their duty to keep us safe, they are cops they have no say.
Just doing the job for which they signed up, trying to help protect us all,
they must be wondering why some of us just want to see them fall.

Who'd be a cop, risking life and limb, putting their lives on the line,
I'm glad that some take that risk and all to keep us fine.
We should all be grateful for the thin blue line, it keeps us safe in our bed,
if they weren't there then who would do their job, who can we trust instead?
Our Bobbies are heroes, who can't win in times like this, don't let the line fall,
let's help and support them, or lose the safety they bring to one and all.

I have worked as an IT supplier to the Police Service for 22 years and during that time, I have been privileged to participate in numerous award ceremonies. The selfless bravery and commitment of these public servants is nothing short of outstanding.

Sir Robert Peel's 2nd Core Idea said "The key to preventing crime is public support. Every community member must share the responsibility of preventing crime, as if they were all volunteer members of the force. They will only accept this responsibility if the community supports and trusts the police".

48. Happy Birthday Dad

What I would give to be able to say, Happy Birthday Dad, you're 90 today,
but he was taken from us many years ago, so it's something I will never say.
My Dad was my hero and I wanted to make him proud, to be the best I could,
when I left to join the Army, he told me not to worry, if I did my best I would.

My Dad had been an orphan who'd lost his mum at birth, left all alone in life,
brought up by kind people who gave him a home and helped reduce his strife.
He knew what it was to have nothing, but it never got him down,
he lived his life with a smile on his face, he never wore a frown.

When he married and had his family, he worked hard to be the best Dad,
to show us how to do things properly, to never be selfish, cruel or bad.
Kind and caring he taught us all well, determined to give us everything he could,
he had lived a life with nothing, so made sure we never would.

As a junior soldier I gave everything, I made boy RSM, so I did my best,
I wanted to show him that I could make it, great training did the rest.
He never made it to my proudest day, but he held my hand throughout,
in my mind he was there, his heart filled with pride, of that I have no doubt.

When I sit and think of him my heart just bursts with pride,
although he left us 45 years ago, he's always by my side.
I hope my Dad is proud of me and how I've lived my life,
I know he would love my caring son and he knew my beautiful
wife.

Sleep tight Dad, I will always love you and know we'll meet
again,
with Mum by your side you'll be waiting, and together forever
we'll all remain.
There's so much time to make up, it's been so many years,
but I know when I get there we'll be together again, no more
tears.

*My Dad was my hero, and I will never get over his loss so many
years ago at the age of 45. I was a very young soldier,
desperate to make his dad proud, but having achieved the rank
of RSM as a junior soldier, he passed before my Graduation
Parade, a Parade that I commanded.*

*Strangely, I felt his presence on that day, willing me to get
things right in front of hundreds of people. I did and it changed
my life. Thanks Dad.*

49. For My Friend JC

When we first met, he made me smile, because of his love of
tea,
this young Yorkshire lad, the one they all called JC.
As I got to know him better, it made me laugh to see,
it wasn't only tea he liked, but anything marked Tetley.

With a great big heart and a ready smile, we grew very close
him and me,
in fact he was like a little brother, the lad we called JC.
A fine soldier and an even better friend, he was a kind and
gentle man,
he never looked for anything more than to be the best you can.

Like all soldiers we went our separate ways, but we never ever
forgot,
that special bond that was between us, is the strongest of the lot.
We were Arctic Warriors, who could climb, fight and ski,
the mate that stood beside me, the one I called JC.

The years passed by, he married Trish, and they raised a family
together,
we only saw each other now and then but our friendship lasted
forever.
The friends that passed before will take good care when he
arrives,
they will lay a place at the table in Valhalla, the place where all
of us will be,
they will put an arm around him, comfort and care for him, my
brother JC.

It's goodnight my friend not goodbye, we'll meet again you see,
till it's my time to join you, I will recall the good times, with
my old pal JC.
When you look down on Trish and the boys, I know you'll be
wearing a smile,
because you will always be with them you're just resting for a
while.

**Goodnight, god bless and sleep well JC; thanks for being my
friend**

*I met Jonathan Craven (JC) around 44 years ago, when he
arrived in the same unit as me. He was a very quiet guy but
still a lot of fun; most of all he was just a good lad and a great
friend. His intake of Tetley's, tea and beer, was a source of
great amusement, and he became like a little brother to me.*

*He was one of these people that just don't have a nasty bone in
their body, always open, honest, and completely transparent.
He died of cancer last year and I know he's upstairs now,
looking down with a Tetley's in his hand.*

50.   Remembrance 2021

I thank the Lord for my service every single day,
for the friends I still have and those I lost along the way.
Where Warriors fell, we brought them home and laid them down to rest,
for these were heroes who died for us, who deserved the very best.

I remember each and every one as if they were still here,
that's because they were my mates, and I will always hold them dear.
As the years roll past and we grow old, they will stay forever young,
we will always see them as they were, healthy, fit and strong.

As they gather in Valhalla, we know they will wait for us there,
to help us make our journey and to offer us their prayer.
We are a band of brothers who don't always get things right,
but we always care for each other and keep our friendships tight.

Their loss lives with us now and it will last for evermore,
until we too have had our time and we step through Valhalla's door.
Our lives have been all the better for our time with these brave men,
they gave their lives for us until we meet again.

Remembering them is easy because they gave their all,
to keep us safe and let us live, forever standing tall.
For our Queen and country their great sacrifice was made,
young men who never grew old, because with their lives they paid.

Rest in Peace lads, God bless you all

Certa Cito

To a soldier the act of remembrance is very special; it recognises the sacrifices made by those that never made it home. To those of us that did make it through, we try to keep their memories alive, to show respect and appreciation for what they did for us.

In reality, we have to live our lives with our comrades in our hearts and minds because there but for the grace of God go any of us. We live for ourselves, our families and for them. We remember them always!

51. For Mam

We know you had to leave us that sad, cold winter's day,
to start upon your journey, to meet dad along the way.
We brought you home to Scotland, a lovely English rose,
it's where your heart would always lie, as Scottish as it goes.

Your love is always with us in each and every way,
your memory strong as ever, despite each passing day.
I hope you're proud of what you see, looking down from up above,
because you gave us everything, that special mother's love.

The wind will blow, the rain will fall, and we shall all grow old,
but you're in our hearts forever mam, your memory strong and bold.
We know you're only sleeping, together with our dad,
it's what you always wanted so it stops us being sad.

Never take your mam for granted, just think of all she's done,
for one day you will turn around and sadly, she'll be gone.
There are no more chances to tell her just how much you care,
you will regret that forever because she isn't there.

My mother was an incredible lady, strong, feisty, and immensely brave. She did so much for me that I can never repay, and that makes me very sad. I urge all men to remember this short poem:

You only have one mother, faithful kind and true,
No other friend in all the world will be so true to you.

52. Goodnight But Never Goodbye

How do you say goodbye to your very best mate,
the one you laughed with, who made you feel just great.
The years slipped by, and we slowly grew older,
our stories got longer and just a bit bolder.
But the laughs and the memories they never diminished,
and some said our stories never quite finished.

Then as I thought, it became very clear,
it's not goodbye because you'll always be near.
So, it's goodnight my friend and not goodbye,
save a place at your side up there on high,
You're in my heart forever and your memory lives on,
so, it's **Goodnigh**t Dai and never **Goodbye.**

*When Dai Jones left this earth, I knew my life would never be
the same. He was more than my best mate, he was my brother
in every way, less birth.*

*His memory will never die, it's just a matter of time till I get my
best pal back.*

53. My Friend Martin

We meet so many people every single day,
some leave a mark upon you, but most just fade away.
For those who met Martin he always left a mark, and let me tell
you why,
because he was an open, decent, and humble man, a truly
fantastic guy.

We spent many years together in some pretty dodgy places,
but we always undertook these tasks with smiles upon our
faces.
I probably never told him how much his friendship meant,
these things go unspoken because friendship's heaven sent.

I really do regret that I never took time to say,
how much I respected and admired him in every kind of way.
Now he's gone there's one thing that I already know,
his memory will never leave me, it will simply never go.

So, it's only goodnight, Martin and it will never be goodbye,
because we'll meet again my friend way up there on high.
Every time I think of you it will surely make me smile,
but sadly I can't have one final wish, to talk with you a while.
Thanks for your friendship over all these many years,
Until we meet again my friend, I'll be I'll be holding back the
tears.

*Martin was a truly great guy, a northern lad who told it as it
was. Bright, articulate, and the sort of bloke who would never
let you down. I was very proud to call him my friend.*

*He and Marian had made a lovely life in Australia and were
approaching retirement; a time to be together and to enjoy the
fruits of their labour. He was taken too early, with so much left
to give. Why is it always the good guys?*

54. Saying Goodbye

As your parting comes your heart will break and you will surely say,
just why did Martin have to leave, why did he go away.
But in your heart you will always know,
he didn't choose to leave, he simply had to go.

The love you shared and the memories can never die,
so, it's only goodnight, Martin and will never be goodbye.
As he sleeps and the years go past you will always know,
he's watching over you, because he loves you so.

He wants you to embrace the life yet to live,
he knows your special with so much yet to give.
To honour your love and enjoy your life,
because that's what he wants for his darling wife.
He will wait in heaven till the time is right,
when you are old and ready to say goodnight.

I couldn't make it to Martin's funeral which was a heartbreaker, but I was lucky enough to be asked by Marian to write a few words, for which I was truly grateful. Martin was a good friend.

He had the heart of a lion, but was still a little bit shy, so I also wrote a poem for Marian to reflect their love for each other. I hope she liked it.

55. The Soldier's Tale

These lads all touched my life Lord and although they may be
gone,
I will always hold them in my heart until my life is done.
Please put your arms around them Lord, for they were all good
men,
please care for them and keep them safe, until we meet again.

Sig Steve Richmond
Cpl Del Wood
SSgt (YofS) Robbie Davies
WO2 (SSM) Pete Griffin
Lt Jim Barry
Cpl Rab Burns
Sgt Mick Newman
SSgt Kev Froggatt
WO2 (RQMS) Steve Simpson
Capt (Tfc) Bob Pemberton

God bless you guys, RIP.

Certa Cito *(Motto of the Royal Corps of Signals)*

*This list represents the great friends I lost during my service;
each one of them was special, and their stories will live on in
my heart.*

*Thanks for your friendship, guys, each of you taught me
something and I will hold on to that for the rest of my life.*

56. My Benjy Boy

For 16 years he stood at my side,
his big brown eyes so full of pride.
His shiny coat, his wagging tail,
his strength and loyalty would always prevail.

Such an amazing thing for all to see,
this beautiful creature's total love for me.
Full of goodness, affection and trust,
returning his love was an absolute must.

When I got home I would always see,
the wagging tail of my little Benjy.
Now he's gone my heart is so sad, I know no joy,
he was my beautiful black lab, my Benjy Boy.

He gave me so much, I was never alone,
for the price of a hug and a gravy bone.
I'll miss him forever, but in my heart, I know,
he'll be waiting for me when it's my time to go.

They say a dog is man's best friend,
more faithful than many could comprehend.
I believe this saying might have been made for me,
and the love I received from my beautiful Benjy.

*Benjy was my black Lab and probably the gentlest thing I have
ever come across in my life. If only people had the spirit this
old boy showed, the world would be a far better place.*

*My life will never be the same without him, but I thank God for
the gift of letting me take care of him for all those years. We
will walk together again one day. I love you, Benj.*

57. The High Street

As we walk down our High Street and wonder just why,
this way of life is going to die.
Forever the place where everything you could get,
killed by that monster we call internet.
Our way of life will change forever,
unless we make a stand to keep it together.

As children we knew it was a place for joy,
the place you went to get yourself a toy.
We hated the walk, but we didn't say,
because we knew when we got there, we'd get our own way.

As teens we'd head off down the street,
in the hope the love of our life we may possibly meet.
In time it would happen, in a cafe, a shop or a store,
putting us together for evermore.
Married with children it was still part of life,
to head down the street, husband, children and wife.

As adults it was real family time, bringing us together in a
lovely way,
despite arguments, tantrums and inevitable strife, it ended in a
special day.
Our families enjoyed their time together on the street,
visiting the shops, restaurants and bars was a treat.
You could spend as you wanted on food, drink or a toy,
but it was being together that gave us the joy.

As the future moves on the High Street seems doomed,
killed by e-commerce as laziness loomed.
We couldn't be bothered to stretch our legs and walk to town,
we'd sit on our arse and let the High Street down.
When it dies, we'll regret that day and what we failed to do,
as the High Street disappears into history for me and you.

Our grand kids will never know the excitement or joy,
of a walk down the street to find that special toy.
A family trip that meant so much will be gone forever,
when all that was needed was to support the High Street
together.

*Blokes are seldom great shoppers, but our High Streets are so
much more than just rows of shops and hold so many memories.
For many of us they have been the backdrop to our lives; the
place where our parents bought us presents.*

*Lots of us met our partners there, went out on Saturday nights
along those streets, yet so many are just dying around us.
Convenience is killing them, so why not get behind them; I'm
sure we will fancy a walk down the street at some point in the
future!*

58. Admit You're Scared

The day you leave I just have to admit,
that last glance at your loved ones is the terrible bit.
We're tough guys of course, so you just don't show,
the pain in your heart as you let your wife's hand go.
Even worse with your kids, it's a terrible pain,
not knowing whether you will ever hold them again.

As we set off to war, there was a lot of bravado on show,
but the self-same guys, didn't really want to go.
They were sons and husbands and many fathers as well,
why would you want to set off for the gates of hell?
But every soldier knows that this is his calling, his role,
to serve Queen and country and to achieve our goal.

Arriving in theatre, and not the one where you watch a show,
you're starring in this one, so you'd better get to know,
how to keep your focus, your eyes wide open even when you're
in bed,
because, as they say in Scotland, "you're a long time dead".
You need to help the local people and to that you hold on,
it takes your mind off your family and how long you've been
gone.

It's not that you're looking to forget your real life,
but more to keep focus so you can return to your wife.
The kids will miss you, but their timeline is confused,
so as long as you come home, they're resilient, even when
bruised.
No man who has been under fire, can tell me they weren't
scared,
it is human nature and they should be proud they dared.

So, when it's all over and the dying is done,
you close your eyes and prey gently for everyone.
Not just your comrades and allies that passed,
but the soldiers of all sides who have breathed their last.
As you walk from the plane, the bus or the train,
you see your loved ones waiting for you, you made it home
again.

*Emotion is a part of us, and an important element of our
humanity. Don't be frightened to show you care, otherwise
your loved ones may believe you don't, and it can be a long way
back from there.*

*Being scared is normal and will play a big part in your ability
to survive. Only fools don't fear death and that multiplies many
times over for those with children. Embrace that fear and use it
as a force for good.*

59. The Scottish Soldier

When I first left home, I was just a boy with a dream,
to join the Army and make my mark in the team.
I was anxious and worried as my train travelled south,
just what had I signed up for, why the dryness in my mouth.
Farther from home than this boy had ever ventured to be,
not knowing whether I chose the Army or the Army chose me.

When we arrived a roll call was taken, to check just who we
were,
lots of shouting in loud voices to confirm we were there.
I wondered who the guy called Greig could be,
but then I realised the Corporal was shouting at me.
My name is George I thought, but of course that was before I
got here,
they reversed my name to sharpen my focus, isn't that a bit
queer.

My time in college changed my life in so many ways,
thinking about others, the team and the plan within days.
There's no "I" in team instructors say, a point that stayed with
me forever,
it underpinned my plan, built up trust, and taught me what was
meant by together.
To get the best out of people and show them how to succeed,
life as a soldier was meant for me, thank God I found it and met
my need.

My military life shaped everything, it made me the man I
wanted to be,
there were tears and sadness when friends fell, into the mouth
of hell I'd see.
Too many good guys didn't come home, lost forever serving
their Queen,
heroes that I will remember, but for their families never again to
be seen.

Born in Scotland, made in the Royal Signals is my cry,
it's the pride of my life and I will always know why.

I was a very happy soldier and always appreciated finding the thing I was born to do. I wish I could say it was planned, but it wasn't, if anything, it found me.

But the moral to this story is simple, when you find something you love doing, give it everything you have got. Grab your opportunities with both hands because nothing lasts forever, and you need to prepare for the next stage of your journey.

60. Be Kind to Each Other

Once famous across the world for our manners, work ethic, and toil,
now our behaviour can be so offensive, we're not wanted on foreign soil.
Is this really what our youth want "British" to mean, do they really not care,
that we are loathed and unwelcome almost everywhere.

We still lead the world in so many places and make our contribution,
a small island nation who will always help to find the best solution.
So, it's only our manners that have truly slipped away,
and if we just show care for others, we could fix it today.
Manners cost nothing as people often point out, so give it a try,
we can quickly regain the status we had in days gone by.

Being kind to others should make us all feel good,
to help our fellow man in the way we all should.
Whether old or frail, fit or strong, giving respect for others is key,
to allowing us all to show how kind and caring we really can be.
Being kind is special and so easy to do,
it says so much about mankind, but especially you.

My parents and grandparents would often say "it costs nothing to be nice" and that is fact. It was a very British comment, but somehow it has been lost along the way.

I urge people to give it a try because it is a therapeutic thing to do, to show care, compassion, and humanity is real strength.

61. The Yeoman Poet

Becoming a Yeoman was a highlight in my life, it filled me up with pride,
when my soldier service ended I felt sad, was that my career on the slide.
From the main man to just another officer, with a pretty naff title,
little did I know what the true benefit would be, or the post so vital;
A Yeoman so long I believed it may actually be my name,
but when I reflect it was just part of the Traffic Officer game.

I have always loved words, but I didn't think I could be a poet,
the simple truth is unless you try, you will never really know it.
It has given me so much over many years, where grief touched my life,
helping to stem the pain and tears, providing a barrier to my strife.
It has taken a long time to feel confident to share,
something so special that can deliver such care.

I decided to re-use my old name "Yeoman", it always felt right,
when seeking to help others it was a trusted handle, short and bright.
I hope people don't think I use this name as an excuse to hide my own,
the use of this handle is close to my heart, and it's only a short-term loan.
Having been a Yeoman fills me with happiness and pride,
I share my poems under that title now, to celebrate my time on that side.

My love of words has been very helpful through two careers and is going to become the centre of my third, as an Author. I write poetry under a pseudonym "The Yeoman Poet" and also used my previous title on my blog "The Yeoman's Blog".

Given a Yeoman of Signals is a master communicator, I thought it was apt!

62. Collaboration

I have always been proud of my nationality and roots,
a Highland Scot who is British to the sole of his boots.
I have served my country all my life, not a single day off did I ask,
first as a soldier then with Blue Lights, doing my bit to deliver the task.

I owe Blue Lights an enormous debt, allowing me to retain my pride,
for letting me help deliver the best public safety services world-wide.
So, I am very aware that my drive for change, may impact many friends,
but we must act now, before this all changes, and the quality ends.

For the size of our land our team is too big, 45 police forces strive away,
then we have our Firefighters, 57 Services fighting fires all day.
Our Ambulance Trusts may have seen the light, 13 may be just about right,
it is surely time to think again, to bring them together to see the light.

Collaboration is the way to go, working smarter to strengthen the frame,
reducing bureaucracy, waste, 100 senior leaders removed from the game.
Good people that have given so much but times change, so structures must,
aligning our services and joining them up, based on need and genuine trust.

It's not about jobs as some claim, but just about improvement for me,
better use of our heroes in a safer way, with a collaborative base we can see.
Our love of "local" I understand, but we can't afford it so we must get real,
it will always cost more to run more teams, so I believe reality to be ideal.

Taking a collaborative approach is so very important in many areas of life. It's particularly relevant in the Emergency Services (ES) world, where the delivery of collaborated Police, Fire, and Ambulance services can make such an impact.

Cross-border incidents become less complex to manage, all appropriate resources are delivered to the right place, individual services can be streamlined, and most importantly, the public purse could save £millions. Please think about this...

63. You Only Have One Mam

Never take your Mam for granted, no matter what the reason may be,
everything she told you or advice she gave, was just to help you see.
You're everything to her a bond that can't be broken, she'll help in any way,
she wants you to be honest, kind and caring, she will trust in what you say.
No one else can show the loyalty a mother offers, every single day,
cherish this bond forever, in childhood and later life, before it's taken away.

When it's time for Mam to go no one will be ready, because of who she is,
your greatest ally, supporter and loyal friend, always there with a kiss.
Most would give anything to have her back, including their right arm,
but remember her advice, be brave, be kind and stay away from harm.
Her advice was always right, so who do you talk to now, who can help today,
The answer comes as your heartache eases, just think what Mam would say.

The lessons she taught are forever, that was always her plan,
she'd thought it through, worked it out, so she will always help where she can.
I am one of the lucky ones, who had my Mam in my life for many years,
as I said at the start, I wasn't ready to lose her so I shed a lot of tears.

The moral of this story though, is she never really left, she just isn't around,
So, I think of her often and consider her advice, it was always really sound.
My final point is simply this, you only have one Mam until her life is done,
take care, love her, you'll miss her when she's gone, I know, I had one.

Mothers are such an integral part of our lives growing up, but the funny thing is we never stop getting older and your mum's advice is never withheld; even when you wish it was!

Cherish that fact and make good use of it because you will really miss it when it's gone.

64. No Respect?

I grew up respecting my elders because that's what I was
taught,
I wonder why this lesson has been lost, is it because now it's
simply not.
Maybe our youngsters don't care so much, too interested in
their screen,
self-obsessed, wanting only what matters to them, or is that just
too mean.
Is this just some form of cover up, to push away the blame?
remember who their teachers are, the clue is in the name.

I think it's time for us to think a little harder about the things we
say,
our youngsters are like every other generation in mostly every
way.
Perhaps respect is decreasing because we lecture as opposed to
teach,
it is something we should consider; I think it's probably within
our reach.
Rather than just point fingers, let's accept our faults and make a
bid,
to show them respect and manners and bring up a real good kid.

My final point is support our youth, give them a chance or on
your bike,
oh, I did forget I have got just one ask of them, please stop
saying like.

I hear only too often how terrible the younger generation is; that's nonsense! I'm not implying that everything is perfect, but rather than continually criticise them, let's show them some respect and support.

I also urge the older generation to remember that we were the tutors, the mentors, the one's showing the example. Did we get it right?

65. What's Happened to Our Union?

When our union has been at its best, it's because we stood side by side,
so why now, in the darkest of times, do we choose not to show our pride.
Our strength was always drawn from a union where joint decisions were made,
for all of us, not just the few, those brave decisions were laid.

British people are being forced apart, why and is it fair,
or is it simply the extension of the musings of a man called Tony Blair.
Devolved government works, I can hear some people say,
it does in simple admin ways but when the chips are down, no way.

We need strong leadership, the Bulldog spirit that sets us apart,
that is only present when we're together, sharing decisions from the heart.
Our four great countries are exactly that, but stronger together we are,
why continually deplete this strength I ask because it has taken us so far.

I'm a British citizen and a Highland Scot, and proud of both. But I fear for our Union and believe that the constant drive for devolution is taking us down the wrong path.

We are stronger together and the dissolution of the greatest Union the world has ever seen is total folly. Let's accept our position as one of the world's most diverse and inclusive countries to build an even greater Britain.

66. What is Religion?

It has so much to answer for and of that there is no doubt,
persecution, death and misery always follow it, around and
about.
So why do people need this thing and claim it to be good, fair
and kind,
when all we ever see and hear is the pain so many find.

But there should be balance to everything right, we all should
take a look,
to see what's behind the stories that will appear inside some sort
of book.
Do the stories help us make sense of life, or improve in any
way?
Take time to think it through and give their message a chance,
because who knows, it may.

I believe everything in moderation, is a trusted path to take,
who knows the lessons you may learn, or great decisions you
may make.
When considering the different paths of course, I ask you to
always mind,
to be open, fair and inclusive in your thoughts, and simply to be
kind.

Avoid talking of religion, a point often raised, but note I gave it
no name,
because that's where it all starts, the hatred and the blame.
Let's all focus on the lessons at the start, I wanted them to
show,
we need to understand each other first and that will tell us
where to go.

I'm not an overtly religious man but I do believe in the human spirit of kindness and decency. I do though feel that all people should be allowed to follow their religion of choice as a basic human right.

My personal issue is that religion can be attributed as a central cause of too many conflicts. That of course is not to lay the blame at religion's door; I just believe we should all be able to live together in harmony and peace.

67. What Were You Born To Do?

Little boys born to play football, girls to marry a prince,
that's what they said in the old days, but things have changed
long since.
Boys prefer to do simple things that let them take life steady,
girls spend their whole life now just simply getting ready.

But many kids are still born to a role they just struggle
sometimes to find it,
where they have a gift, a special skill but never a chance to
show their bit.
The worst is when the chance is lost to show how good they
are,
talent is lost, lives are lessened, and these talents are left in a
jar.

What a gift it is to never have doubt on what you were born to
do,
a great position for lucky folk don't you wish it was me and
you.
To be honest though, I can't hide my pride and have to admit
I'd seen,
what I was born to do very early on in the service of my Queen.

*I think we would all like to do something we love as work. Very
few of us get that chance, but then again, how many of us know
what it is and actively go seeking it?*

*From my perspective, the most important thing is to take
control of our own destiny: don't let anybody tell you "You
can't", because you can do anything you set your mind to.*

68. Women are Better Drivers

You can hear the advice can't you, move over a bit love don't
hog the road,
straighten up a bit you're drifting in endless commentary mode.
Check your mirrors, indicate there's a car right up your back,
if you don't pick up your speed we're bound to get a crack.

This of course is just general chat because he needs to keep you
straight,
you're a woman not a bloke, so you're used to the constant
grate.
He assumes his mileage tops your skills even with his points
and a fine,
there's never a minute in which he might think, he may have
crossed the line.

The truth is usually simple but it's often just too hard to take,
when you point out to a bloke that woman drive better, just
listen to the excuses they make.
There shouldn't be too many surprises, this is a case of fact we
can't hide,
but it's usually just bravado that challenges the point, we blokes
guard our pride.

*OK guys, this might be hard to take, but I feel it is a simple
truth, women are better drivers! Perhaps it's down to lower
levels of aggression, maybe it's just down to patience, but I
suspect it's more sinister than that.*

*It's much more likely to be the machismo angle, my car's faster
than your thing: frankly, I don't care. Grow up!*

69. The Home Team

I have always wondered why footie fans support teams from far
away,
surely it's right to support your own club, who come from
where you stay.
Maybe it's tribal or because it just doesn't make sense to me,
to see local people wear kits from another team, that's not good
to see.

I know success is what attracts people to support a winning
team,
are we really that shallow I ask, what about the local dream?
What happened to "it's about taking part not winning",
don't answer that, it's too hard to consider without grinning.

Am I a true fan I really don't know, but if not, I have got life
wrong,
my team are what gives me local pride, I believe in the words of
our song.
If it's just about winning, I don't think it's real, it not what
matters to me,
stand free is our call, red is our colour and that's the difference
you see.

*Support your home team, it represents your town or area and
should be a source of local pride. Too many people chase the
success and don't really care about where the team is based;
that's a shame.*

*Football is our national game, and the teams represent the
locality, so let's get back to brass tacks here. No more Man
Utd supporters from London. And for Scotland, it doesn't have
to be a 2-club race.*

70. How to Save Old Folk

I've always respected my elders, enjoyed the stories they tell,
if you look closely when they speak you will note a smile as
well.
Because this helps them play their role in life, to add their little
bit,
much better than spending their life with nothing to do but sit.

As I myself grew older it became much clearer to me,
the damage that is inflicted when old people can no longer be,
part of the discussion, the planning and getting themselves into
gear,
scarily, it's often nothing to do with their health just the
inability to hear.

I often watched the impact this dreadful infliction would create,
stealing their pride in a silent world to which we simply can't
relate.
You can see the "help me" signs in their eyes, but you quickly
see why,
if you can't get them re-engaged, they'll fade away and die.

So please don't believe it's always sickness that takes our old
folk away,
often it's nothing more than sitting in a chair all day.
They have lots to offer the world and they need to be part of the
team,
help to defeat this silent world, it doesn't matter if you have to
scream.

It's a personal belief I hold and I'm no Doctor I know,
but if sat in a chair, people talking around you, wouldn't you
decide to go!

I have witnessed the effect of people being "cut off" because of age related hearing problems, and it is very sad to see. Perfectly lucid, intelligent people that suddenly find themselves ignored, because it's easier than trying to engage them; the result is they start to believe their life is over.

Don't let that happen, help them and keep them engaged. Speak up!

71. Change Your Day

When you wake up in the morning,
try not to think in a cynical way.
There's enough bad news out there so take a different view,
let's look for the positives in life, what would be good for you.

It's just too easy to lie in bed and all you have to say,
is it's just another morning, the start of a miserable day.
What is it you want from life, what can you give back?
it's so much more fun to think this way than simply just attack.

There's a whole wide world out there and it's full of good and
bad,
but you have the chance to change things and for that you
should be glad.
Take a great big breath, get out of bed and put a spring in your
step,
many folks have real issues, they're ill, poor or in debt, so you
can be their rep.

So, today's the day you can start afresh, where you can play a
part,
in helping all those other folk and show that you've got heart.
Now that's what life is all about don't just watch it go by, live,
you're important, you are strong, and you've got a lot to give.

*Life is good, fact. Rather than focus on your problems, try to
think of the positive aspects of life. Most people in the modern
world, me included, have no experience of genuine hardship.*

*A roof over your head, food on the table, and work to pay the
bills? If you can answer yes to those things, the rest is up to
you.*

72. I Miss My Dog

First thing in the morning I reach out from my bed,
I leave my hand there lingering, just feeling for his head.
But it isn't there and that makes me sad, the world is not the same,
since my Benjy left me and I can't shout out his name.

He's been gone so very long I ought to know by now,
there is no point in dreaming he can't come home no how.
He's just a dog my friends would say not meaning to be unkind or bad,
they just didn't understand the amazing bond we had.

Getting home has never been the same since Benjy left my side,
no happy little content face when the door swings open wide.
It always felt so special then how did he know when I pulled up,
I thought about it many times, but he could do it as a pup.

All the years I'd waited, to ensure the time was right,
to go and get my pup and bring him up so bright.
People said he had a fantastic long life, there's no point being bereft,
but I can't understand how life just carries on when my little Benjy's left.

I write a lot about my dog, Benjy. He's been gone for 14 years but I miss him every day; he was a huge part of my life and that of my family. He never sulked, was never grumpy, and just taking him out for a walk was like us winning the lottery.

If we could be that happy the world would be a very different place!

73. Am I a Moonraker Now?

I've been in Wiltshire a very long time and I feel its home to
me,
when people ask where I'm from I will show my pride you see.
I'm a Scot who lives in Wiltshire, but the county's my home
now,
I know it so well after all these years, I can show folks just how.

My mates often note my love and very genuine pride,
for this special place in which I live, this beautiful countryside.
It wraps itself around our lives, helps us overcome the stresses
life can bring,
when you live in gorgeous Wiltshire, it'll make your heart sing.

But here's the critical question, am I a Scot or a Wiltshire man,
and it tickles me to think I can be either one, I can.
There are plenty places in this world that I've had the pleasure
to see,
there can never be any doubt though that Scotland's home to
me.

With that one fixed now, I need to expand my plan,
I still live in Wiltshire, so that makes me a Wiltshire man.
I may never be a Moonraker and I'm sad about that you see,
it's possible to be more than just one thing, and that kinda
works for me.

For as much as I love Scotland, I will always be grateful for my time in Wiltshire. For years I would travel home on a Friday night from every corner of the UK, but as soon as I crossed the county border it made me smile.

It's a place of immense beauty, where my home stands and my family lived in peace and happiness. I may never be a Moonraker, but I always felt welcome and very much at home. Thank you.

74. Our Queen

Role models are what we need to show us all the way,
people we can look up to at any time of the day.
There aren't many of them though because when you call them
out,
very few step forward, or are ready to bring things about.

Unlike the rest of the world the UK's role model can always be
seen,
she's been there for us always, she's Her Majesty the Queen.
Old but wise, strong but fair she carries her people, leads from
the front,
it's an example that most leaders could learn from, without me
being too blunt.

Thank you, ma'am, we know you care and that you'll never
forget,
your role in life, your people's needs or the example you need
to set.
You shine a light on how it's done and for that we owe you a
debt,
but you'll never call it in because the throughout your life that's
the standard you have set.

*I'm proud to be a royalist and to have served my Queen and
country. I believe our late monarch to be one of the greatest
leaders that has ever lived. Her Majesty Queen Elizabeth II has
given her life to us, her people, with humility, kindness, and
grace.*

God Save the Queen.

75. Words in Rhyme

I love the way that words can rhyme and the synergy you can get,
when you bind these words together, with the patterns that you set.
It's a lovely feeling when you find words that fit the need,
they let you tell your story in a way that lights it up and others will take heed.

I like the fact that I own these words, but it also makes me smile,
when I consider that they belong to us all and I'm just borrowing them a while.
Words can be so helpful when your spirit needs a boost, or when feeling down,
they will bring you comfort, where you struggle to resist a frown.

So don't let your troubles build up or the world get in your way,
life can only get better if you take control and smile another day.
Words are free to use and there's plenty, they really do abound,
write them down and use them, to turn your life around.

Being a storyteller has brought me great happiness over the years, but it has also brought me great peace and comfort in times of loss. I see poetry as just another form of storytelling, but in rhyme. It's amazingly poignant and healing to put your feelings into a poem.

One of my ambitions is to become a prolific poet and to see one of my poems of remembrance hang in my Corps' Museum.

76. Lockdown Lessons

There are always lessons in everything we do, but most of us will say,
it's about making sure we learn them and don't just brush them all away.
Mankind has never felt this pain, or seen suffering on this scale,
where the enemy is invisible and we can't fight back, to stop it in its trail.

But whilst we have to dig to find some good, there will be positives for sure,
our lives will slow for the common good, to make our world more pure.
We show more care for others and do things we didn't normally do,
like knock on a stranger's door to ask, is everything all right with you.

We put others first and often check that they are not forgotten,
that they have food and water, and their supplies have not gone rotten.
It's not just about me, me, me, as things often used to show,
we're starting to truly care again and that's the way to go.

Lockdown has been horrible, it has stripped away our freedom and our rights,
but when you balance up, you realise it hasn't won it's only for a few nights.
The losses endured will forever break our heart, remember this fight we're in,
we'll learn the lessons and won't let our loved ones down, because COVID will never win.

As a society we suffered so much during the pandemic, but it also showed how resilient we are as people. Many families lost loved ones, but they never bowed to COVID, they kept fighting back.

Now in the name of those who lost their lives we must ensure that lessons are learnt, so that in the future we are better prepared. In honour of those that died we must try to make the world a more tolerant, inclusive, and caring place.

77. My Wife

I thought I'd take a moment, to talk of the important things in life,
so, I'll kick it off with the number one thing, my darling lady wife.
We've been together through thick and thin and over many years,
but our marriage has only grown stronger, of that I have no fears.

We'll have been married for 40 years in just twelve months' from now,
what an achievement that will be and I'm proud that we knew how.
I hope she understands, just how much she means to me,
it's really important because, I don't tell her enough you see.

Life together is about love and sharing, patience is an important part,
because we are only human, and we tend to think from our heart.
Make no mistake I'll always know, the fantastic choice I made that day,
when I asked this girl to marry me, she's been by my side all the way.

I would never want any other lass, than the one I was blessed to marry,
it would take me the rest of my life to explain, how happy I was to carry,
my beautiful wife across the threshold, setting off on our journey in life,
blessed indeed and I know it, I can't wait for the rest of our time, me and my darling wife.

Marriage has always been something that I believe in totally; to love somebody with every part of your soul is a true blessing. That, together with being a parent is what I cherish most in life.

I hope I have been a good husband and father, but I will keep on trying to improve because nobody is perfect, certainly not me.

78. My Son

Does any father really know how he'll react, when that special day arrives?
the one where he drives in a trance, desperate to see his baby alive.
He forgets the basic rules of the road, and hopefully doesn't get done,
arriving there to hear, congratulations mate, you've got yourself a son.
It happened to me forty years ago, in a faraway foreign land,
but the Doctor spoke in English and his message was just grand.

I'm a dad I thought and I wanted to scream, I love that wee boy so much,
I knew a special bond would form as our hands came into touch.
How can I be the best dad I think, how do I play that part,
not any little boy, he's the apple of your eye, the one who steals your heart.

To be a father is special, I only got one chance you see,
so, I hope you think I did ok son, because you're everything to me.
Thanks for being the son I always wanted, for being my very best mate,
it means everything to me when you're by my side, that pride will never abate.

The two best things in my life have been getting married and becoming a father. These are the things that drove me to give my best in life and for which I am most thankful.

Being the best I could be was always my challenge to myself and if I have gotten anywhere close, it is because of the love and support of my wife and son. How lucky am I?

79. Keep It Simple

Simple is underrated, I've known that throughout my life,
but some people love complexity, despite the trouble and the
strife.
If it's easy don't make it hard, I can hear myself shout out,
because that's where your time and costs fall down, that's what
it's all about.

Simple can be clever, where complex can be dumb,
that's a message that you'll never get through to some.
It doesn't make it better just because it's hard to do,
it probably just takes longer, more work for me and you.

So don't dismiss simple just to be considered clever,
we need to keep it in our minds, or it will be lost forever.
Simple is as simple does, they use that phrase to scare us some,
but give it a try and you'll see why, it's there to help us
overcome.

*Why do lots of people look down on anything simple? It
sometimes feels as if there is a preference for adding
unnecessary layers of complexity and the reasoning behind that
has always alluded me.*

*I am, have been and always will be an advocate for keeping
things simple. I have witnessed too many instances of the
impact of unnecessarily complex actions, the majority of which
have occurred to satisfy the self-importance of others.*

80. Political Nonsense

People play political games from which they should stay away,
armchair politicians, I can hear so many say.
They always have the answers, but don't ask them for a fact,
for they haven't got a clue of course, they're only there to react.

If you're going to make a point, take time to check it out,
or you'll end up looking silly, no clue what you're talking
about.
There's nothing wrong with opinions, that's the law of our land,
we each should feel the right to speak, not bury our head in the
sand.

If you like politics of course, then stick to what the
professionals say,
they can talk on any point and make it last all day.
But analyse their responses and you'll quickly see through their
game,
they didn't give an answer they just spoke a lot, and kept within
a frame.

*It is probably a mark of my own failings, but I have never liked,
or particularly respected politicians. Personal honesty drives
me to admit that people that operate under the pretence of
serving their country and the public, but often have little
interest beyond their own personal status are not good for
society.*

*It's easy to be critical of course, but the fact that the cream of
our society could never be tempted to enter politics or have
sufficient desire to want to run the country says it all.*

Acknowledgement

I am still a relatively new Author and I see poetry as a simple
extension of storytelling but doing so in rhyme. My love of
words is driving me to continue, so I wrote these poems for my
family because they have given me so much, and I want to
recognise that without them I may have struggled to find the
inspiration. I don't think they would mind me expanding on
that point and in doing so I would simply say thanks to my mam
because I never said it enough. My final thank you is to one of
my teachers, in a little Highland school, Mrs Molly Williamson,
who gave me some great advice 50 years ago that I have only
just put into practice. Good advice sticks with you, so thank
you. I hope people enjoy my work and gain the same comfort
from words as I have done throughout my lifetime.

George Greig

Ingram Content Group UK Ltd.
Milton Keynes UK
UKHW010805190623
423681UK00015B/647